D0998764

LIZARDS

By S.L. Hamilton

Published by ABDO Publishing Company, 8000 West 78th Street, Suite 310, Edina, MN 55439. Copyright ©2010 by Abdo Consulting Group, Inc. International copyrights reserved in all countries. No part of this book may be reproduced in any form without written permission from the publisher. A&D Xtreme™ is a trademark and logo of ABDO Publishing Company.

Printed in the United States of America, North Mankato, Minnesota.
102009
012011

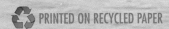 PRINTED ON RECYCLED PAPER

Editor: John Hamilton
Graphic Design: Sue Hamilton
Cover Design: John Hamilton
Cover Photo: Getty Images
Interior Photos: AP-pgs 3, 4, 28, & 29; Getty Images-pgs 1, 6, 7, 12, 13, 14, 15, 18, 20, 21, 22, 23, 30, & 31; iStockphoto-pgs 24, 25, & 32; National Geographic-4 & 5; Peter Arnold-pgs 18 & 19; PhotoResearchers-pgs 8, 9, 10, 11, & 15; and Visuals Unlimited-pgs 16, 17, 26, & 27.

Library of Congress Cataloging-in-Publication Data

Hamilton, Sue L., 1959-
   Lizards / S.L. Hamilton.
      p. cm. -- (Xtreme predators)
   Includes index.
   ISBN 978-1-60453-992-9
   1. Lizards--Juvenile literature. I. Title.
   QL666.L2H27 2010
   597.95--dc22
                              2009043579

CONTENTS

XTREME

LIZARDS

Komodo dragons are the world's largest living lizards, reaching 10 feet (3 m) in length. They can be found on the Indonesian island of Komodo. Adult Komodo dragons can eat more than 100 pounds (45 kg) of meat in a single meal.

Xtreme Quote

"Here there be dragons."
~Early mariners' maps warning of dragons on the islands of Indonesia

A KOMODO'S

6

MOUTH

A Komodo dragon's saliva is filled with deadly bacteria. A bite transfers the bacteria into the prey. Even if the victim escapes, it is only a matter of time before the animal dies of infection.

Teeth

A Komodo dragon's mouth is filled with serrated teeth. They are similar to sharks' teeth. Komodo dragons use their knife-like teeth to rip and saw off large chunks of meat from their prey, which they swallow whole. They do not chew.

A Komodo dragon tooth.

Komodo teeth are hidden in their gums. They often have to bite through their own gums to eat.

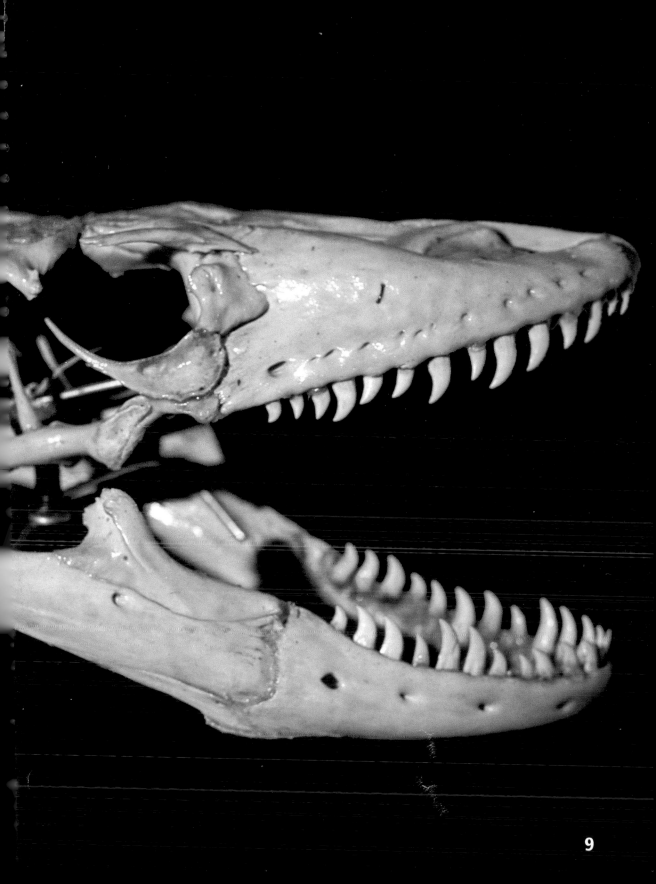

9

Komodo dragons can eat up to 80 percent of their own body weight at one time.

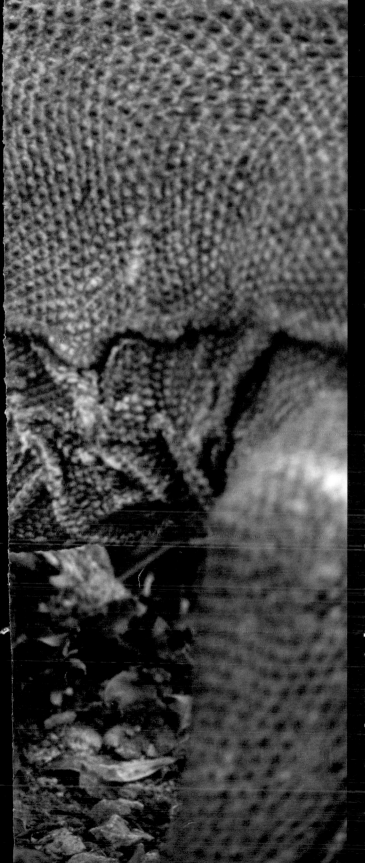

Komodo dragons
hunt patiently,
sometimes waiting
days for their prey
to die. But once
a meal is in front
of them, these
carnivores are
greedy eaters. A
Komodo's mouth
has moveable joints.
The flexible hinges
allow the lower
jaw to open extra
wide. Huge pieces of
meat slide down its
throat and into its
expandable stomach.

TASTE

Komodo dragons eat any kind of meat, swallowing everything from eggs to water buffalo. They particularly like carrion (dead animals). A Komodo uses its specialized forked tongue to find its meals. The tongue picks up chemical molecules on the ground and in the air. The chemicals are transferred to pads on the bottom of the dragon's mouth. Information is then sent to the lizard's brain, and the hunt begins.

Xtreme Fact Komodos can smell a meal up to 5 miles (8 km) away.

& SMELL

BODY &

ARMOR

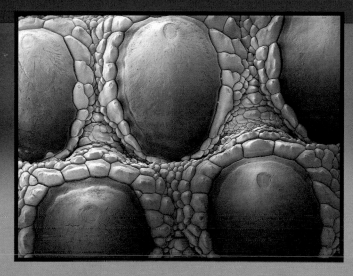

Komodo dragons have short, powerful bodies. Their skin is a tough, scaly armor. They have muscular legs, which allow them to run at speeds of 9 to 11 miles per hour (14-18 kph) over short distances.

Swimming For Their Lives

Komodo dragons
are great swimmers.
Their strong tails
move back and
forth, propelling the
dragons through
the water. If food
becomes scarce,
dragons have been
known to swim to
other islands to
locate prey. Once on
shore, the powerful
tail is used to knock
down prey.

Claws and Tails

Dragons use their long claws to grab and rip up prey. Young Komodos use their claws to climb trees. Trees offer the small lizards protection from large birds, snakes, wild dogs, and even adult Komodos. Full-grown dragons are too big to climb trees, but they use their tails to balance themselves on their hind legs and reach up for food.

OTHER

While the Komodo dragon is the biggest monitor lizard, there are many other species. These predators are found throughout Asia, the islands of Indonesia, and Australia. Most are meat eaters, although some are omnivores, eating both vegetation and meat.

X treme Fact ▷ Perenties are the largest lizards living in Australia. They reach up to 8 feet (2.4 m) in length.

MONITORS

A perentie makes a goanna its next meal.

GILA

Gila monsters (pronounced HEE-la) live in Mexico and the southwestern United States. Although only about 1- to 2-feet long (.3- to .6-m) and slow, these predator lizards have powerful jaws and a venomous bite.

MONSTERS

X treme Quote

"A person would have to be pretty stupid and almost purposely intent on picking up a Gila monster to be bitten by one."
~Arizona Leisure

eating eggs, frogs, and small mammals like mice and rabbits. Only in self-defense will a Gila monster bite a human. But once a Gila monster bites, it does not willingly let go. It clamps down on its victim and delivers its venom by chewing the poison into the flesh.

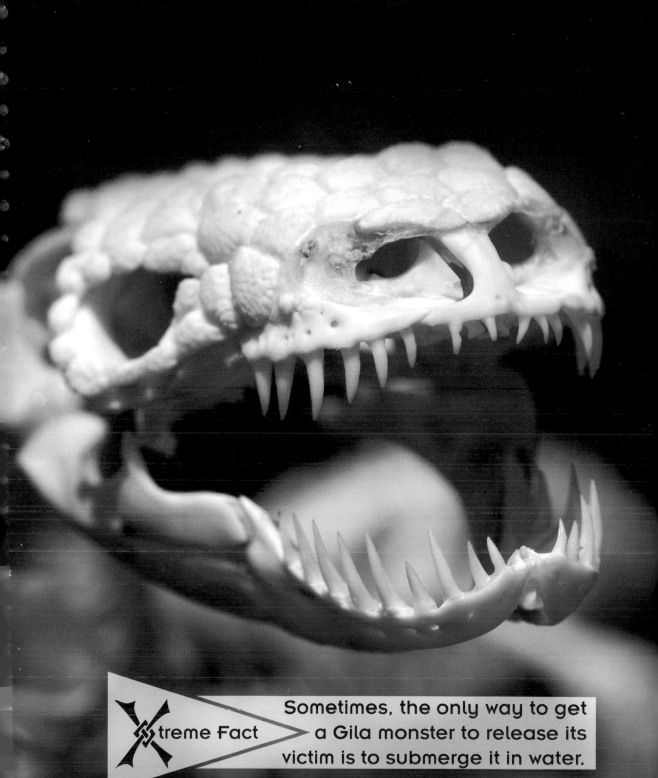

Xtreme Fact Sometimes, the only way to get a Gila monster to release its victim is to submerge it in water.

MEXICAN BEADED

The Mexican beaded lizard is quite similar in looks and attitude to its smaller cousin, the Gila monster. Both chew venom into their victims, and both avoid contact with humans.

LIZARDS

Xtreme Fact

Only about 200 Mexican beaded lizards remain in the wild.

LIZARD ATTACKS ON HUMANS

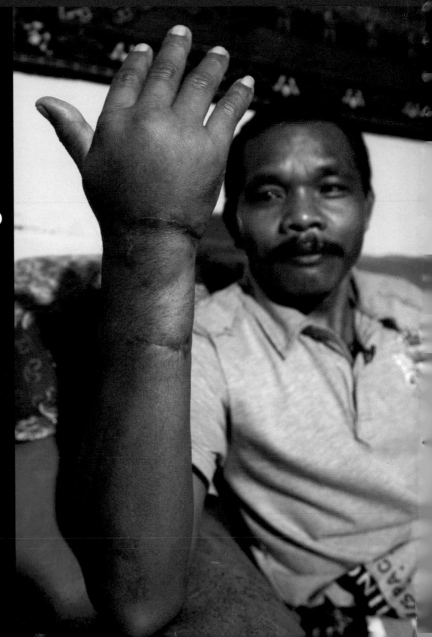

A park ranger in Indonesia shows his wound and swollen hand from a Komodo dragon attack. Although rare, venomous lizards do attack people, causing serious, life-threatening wounds.

HUMAN ATTACKS ON LIZARDS

Many lizards have been hunted to protect human populations, threatening the great predators with extinction. Another threat is the smuggling of the animals for sale as exotic pets.

THE

Bacteria
Organisms that multiply rapidly and often cause sickness and sometimes death in animals.

Carnivore
An animal that eats other animals.

Carrion
The dead flesh of animals that are decaying.

Exotic Pets
A rare or unusual animal that is kept as a pet.

Indonesia
A country in southeast Asia made up of 17,508 islands, including Java, Sumatra, Borneo, New Guinea, and Komodo Island.

Omnivore
An animal that eats both plants and meat.

GLOSSARY

Predator
An animal that hunts, kills, and eats other animals.

Saliva
A watery liquid found in the mouth. The liquid helps with chewing and swallowing food.

Serrated
Notched like the edge of a saw. Komodo dragons have jagged, serrated teeth, which allow them to rip off big chunks of meat.

Venom
A poisonous liquid that some reptiles such as Gila monsters, snakes, and scorpions use for killing prey, and for defense.

INDEX